Jimmy Wales and Wikipedia

INTERNET BIOGRAPHIES™

Jimmy Wales and Wikipedia

SUSAN MEYER

ROSEN PUBLISHING®
New York

Published in 2013 by The Rosen Publishing Group, Inc.
29 East 21st Street, New York, NY 10010

Copyright © 2013 by The Rosen Publishing Group, Inc.

First Edition

Library of Congress Cataloging-in-Publication Data

Meyer, Susan, 1986–
Jimmy Wales and Wikipedia/Susan Meyer.
    pages cm.—(Internet biographies)
Includes bibliographical references and index.
ISBN 978-1-4488-6912-1 (library binding)
1. Wales, Jimmy—Juvenile literature. 2. Wikipedia—Juvenile
literature. 3. Electronic encyclopedias—Juvenile literature. 4.
Businesspeople—Biography—Juvenile literature. I. Title.
AE100.M49 2013
030.92—dc23
[B]
                                                    2011048590

Manufactured in the United States of America

CPSIA Compliance Information: Batch #S12YA: For further information, contact Rosen Publishing, New York, New
York, at 1-800-237-9932.

Contents

INTRODUCTION

If you've ever done research for a project online or searched for more information about nearly anything, you've probably come across an article on a Web site called Wikipedia. In fact, so many people visit the Web site Wikipedia.org each day that it is ranked among the top ten sites in the world. No other encyclopedia or reference site comes close to Wikipedia's daily Web traffic or overall popularity. Traditional encyclopedias are printed and bound. However, because it is a Web site that updates constantly with new information, Wikipedia can provide more up-to-the-minute information than any other encyclopedia.

But how does Wikipedia manage to have information so quickly and on such a wide range of subjects? It is because thousands of people volunteer their time to write and edit articles on Wikipedia. In fact, anyone who wants to can edit an article. For this reason, you may have heard teachers or librarians say that Wikipedia is not a good source to use for papers or projects. The downside of letting anyone update an article is that someone might update it with incorrect information. You don't always know where the information is coming from or how accurate it is.

While this may be true, it is also fair to say that Wikipedia has truly revolutionized how we access information. In just a decade since its founding, Wikipedia has managed to eclipse every other encyclopedia in the world in nearly every language. But where did this highly successful Web site come from? Who came up with the idea of an encyclopedia that would be entirely written and edited by a world of Internet users? Inspired by similar ideas and through his lifetime of experiences, the man who is primarily credited with the idea for Wikipedia is its founder, Jimmy Wales.

From a small town in Alabama, Jimmy Wales used his strong education, knowledge, and personal philosophy that information should be free and open to all people to create the Web site Wikipedia. With the help of several friends and colleagues he met along the way, Wales was able to create something truly unique that has changed the way we research and learn about the world.

It's hard to imagine a world without Wikipedia. No matter what subject you look up on search engines across the Internet—from velociraptors to Calvin Coolidge to Azerbaijan—frequently it is a Wikipedia article that surfaces as the top result. Almost without fail, Wikipedia

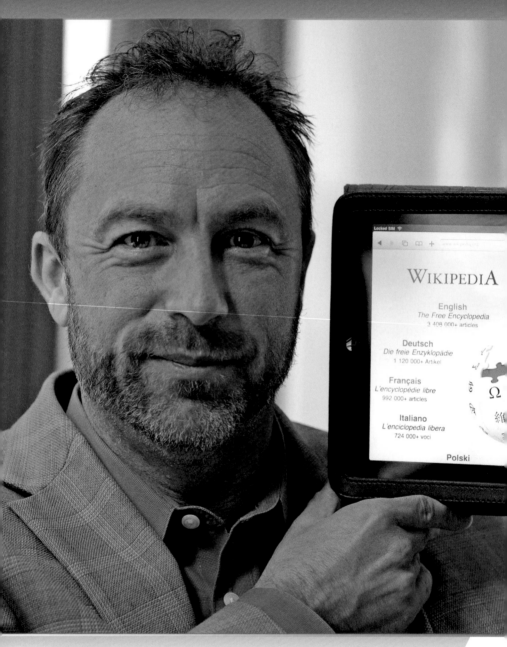

Jimmy Wales is seen displaying the homepage for Wikipedia, the free online encyclopedia he helped to create, on an iPad. This photo was taken in Hamburg, Germany, during an interview with Wales about the Web site.

will show up at least in the top five results. And not just in English—the Web site currently holds articles in 282 languages, from Sanskrit to Inuktitut. A devoted community of volunteers around the world works together to create an extensive encyclopedia that is free for everyone.

This book examines the life of the man responsible for those inevitable search engine hits. Jimmy Wales is still a fairly young man, but he has accomplished much in his life. This book will look at the events and people in his life that led to his success as well as what he is currently doing with his life—both with Wikipedia and with new ideas. It will also take an in-depth look at Wales's lasting legacy, the giant of a Web site that transformed the way we share and create information on the Internet: Wikipedia.

CHAPTER 1

Early Life and Education

Jimmy Wales, who would one day take the world by storm by creating the immensely popular Web site Wikipedia, was not born in a large city or center of technology. He was born in Huntsville, Alabama, on August 7, 1966. The population of Huntsville at the time Wales was born was around one hundred thousand, making it the fourth-largest city in Alabama. However, prior to 1960, the population was only around twenty thousand. What accounted for this great boom right around the time of Wales's birth? Although Alabama was, and is today, generally known as an agricultural center rather than a technological one, around this time Huntsville became the center of a very technological industry: space exploration.

Around 1960, an event called the Cold War was happening between the United States and the Soviet Union. The Cold War was a competition—rather than a series of battles with guns—to see who would have the most

The World Book Encyclopedia

When Jimmy was only three, his mother bought a set of the *World Book Encyclopedia* from a traveling salesman. *World Book* was a popular set for families at the time because the thick glossy pages and black-and-white photographs made it both more durable and more accessible to children than the other, more academic encyclopedias of the time.

As Jimmy learned to read, he became fascinated by the encyclopedia and the amount of information available to him just by turning its pages. But while young Jimmy loved to read the *World Book*, he also saw some limitations to its usefulness. He could see right in his hometown that things were changing very quickly in the world. Whole sets of encyclopedias were too expensive for individual families to buy a new set every year. To help update the information, World Book would send out stickers to all the encyclopedia owners. Jimmy remembers applying the stickers to the book. Unfortunately, this could work for only so long before a new edition would need to be purchased.

Little did Doris Wales know that by buying an encyclopedia for her young son, she would help spark an idea that would change the world.

advanced technology. A big part of the Cold War was the "space race" to see who could make the greatest advances in space travel. Soon, space centers began to spring up around the country. Because of the way gravitational forces work, it is better to launch rockets from a spot closer to the equator. Additionally, the ideal place to launch rockets will also have wide-open spaces. Consequently, Alabama, with its location in the southern United States and its abundance of farmland, was an ideal spot. Almost

Huntsville, seen here, is the fourth-largest city in Alabama. According to the 2010 census, its population is over 180,000, but when Wales was born there, back in 1966, it was considerably smaller.

overnight the small town of Huntsville became a bustling city when the Redstone Arsenal and Marshall Space Flight Center opened there. The space center poured resources and academics into the area. Huntsville soon earned the nickname "Rocket City."

It was in the middle of all this hubbub and major technology boom that Jimmy Wales was born. Many people assume that his real name is James and that Jimmy is only a nickname; however, his official name is actually

Jimmy. He and his three siblings (of which he is the oldest) grew up to the sounds of rocket tests being done in the

This sign welcoming visitors and residents stands outside the Redstone Arsenal. This U.S. space and rocket center caused a huge boom in Huntsville's population right around the time Wales was born.

background of the growing city. Wales told a reporter from a local Alabama paper called the *News Courier* in 2006

about how growing up in Huntsville around this time had an effect on his views on science and technology: "It had a very interesting influence on me. Growing up in Huntsville during the height of the space program, and all the exciting things going on with that, kind of gave you an optimist view of the future, of technology and science."

THE IMPORTANCE OF EDUCATION

Wales's parents were both strong believers in the importance of a good education for their children. His father, Jimmy Wales Sr., was the manager of a local grocery store. His mother, Doris Wales, ran a small school with the help of

Jimmy's grandmother, Erma. The school was called the House of Learning Elementary School, and it operated as a one-room schoolhouse where students from all different grades learned side by side. There were as few as four students in each grade.

Jimmy became a student at the House of Learning. The school followed a philosophy similar to a Montessori school. A Montessori education focuses on the students' independence and self-sufficiency, freedom without boundaries, and respect for the students' psychological welfare and upbringing. Jimmy benefited from the close instruction that allowed for a lot of one-on-one attention. He also gained valuable knowledge by learning from older students. These factors would lead him later in life to champion the one-room schoolhouse model and credit his mother's institution and the early education he received there with much of his later success. He continued to be a student at the House of Learning through the eighth grade.

Jimmy did well in school and got excellent grades. When it came time to advance to high school, he enrolled at a private school in Huntsville known as the Randolph School. The Randolph School was a private prep school. It was a well-respected school, and one of its many advantages was access to computers. Jimmy was able to take his first lessons in computer programming during his time at the Randolph School. This was an extreme rarity in 1979.

At this time, the personal computer was not something that many people owned as they do today. Because of the many advantages it offered its students, the Randolph School was very expensive. However, Jimmy's parents were willing to make sacrifices for their son's education. In an interview for the C-SPAN series *Q&A*, Wales said of his parents philosophy on education: "[My parents] felt that education was important, it was always a passion in my household...the very traditional approach to knowledge and learning and establishing that as a base for a good life."

Jimmy did very well at the Randolph School. He was never ashamed of being a great student and good with computers. In fact, he describes himself in high school as a "geek." Jimmy did so well at Randolph that he graduated from high school when he was only sixteen.

COLLEGE LIFE AND AFTER

After graduating, Wales enrolled in college. He went to Auburn University, which is a state-funded school in the far southeastern part of Alabama. Auburn is about a four-hour drive from Wales's hometown of Huntsville. Wales had always been interested in math and numbers, so he decided to study finance at Auburn. While an undergrad at Auburn, Wales read an essay that he later said would impact his thinking and management of Wikipedia. The essay was called "The Use of Knowledge in Society," and it was by an Austrian economist named Friedrich von Hayek. In this essay, Hayek argued that no single person knows the sum total of the world's information. Rather, each person knows a small fraction of the world's knowledge, and it is through pooling knowledge that people are successful. While absorbing these ideas and influences, Wales continued to enjoy studying and learning. He graduated with an undergraduate degree in finance from Auburn and immediately entered a Ph.D. program at the University of Alabama in Tuscaloosa to continue to pursue his finance studies.

Around this time, Wales also married for the first time. At the age of twenty, he married a local girl from his hometown in Alabama, named Pam. He had met her while they were both working at a local grocery store in Huntsville. Although their marriage was not made to last forever, they stayed friends for many years after they divorced. Pam describes Jimmy in his early twenties as a very ambitious young man, always looking forward to success in his future. Pam said he once showed her a photograph of an English castle and promised her that they would have that one day.

While in his personal life Wales experienced both a marriage and a divorce, in his academic life he continued to plow ahead with his postgraduate studies. Wales left the program at the University of Alabama with a master's

Austrian-born political economist Friedrich August von Hayek won the Nobel Prize for Economics in 1974. Wales studied his work in college and said that it influenced how he ran Wikipedia.

degree in finance. He was still interested in finishing a Ph.D., however, and so he soon entered a second Ph.D. program. This time, Wales took his education outside of Alabama. He attended a program in finance at Indiana University in Bloomington, Indiana. He completed the coursework there but never wrote his dissertation. This meant that he couldn't graduate with a doctorate in finance. Wales said he didn't write the dissertation because he was bored. While in school, Wales did write and publish an academic paper on a complicated aspect of finance: options pricing theory. This paper would soon come to be very helpful as he began to look outside the academic world and turn his focus on the very important task of getting a job.

CHAPTER 2

Early Career and Blossoming Success

In 1994, at the age of twenty-eight, Jimmy Wales walked into the office of the Chicago Options Associates, a well-known financial firm, and met with its chief executive officer, Michael Davis, to interview for a job. Having left Indiana University behind with an unfinished degree, Wales was more than ready to stop studying finance and start applying it to a career. He wanted to put his talent for numbers and mathematics to a practical application: making money.

He had written many extensive papers during his years studying finance in various degree programs. One of these papers was on options pricing theory. Options pricing theory is a very theoretical approach to deciding the fair value of an option or stock. The paper was a very mathematical look at a complicated subject matter. Since he had a certain expertise in finance from a theoretical background, Wales decided the best place to go to pursue a career would be the booming business-rich city of Chicago. Not only did this move allow him to stay in the Midwest and move to a bigger city, but at this time Chicago was one of the biggest centers of the financial industry.

Additionally, Wales happened to have a friend working at the Chicago trading firm Chicago Options Associates where he would soon interview. Knowing about Wales's background in finance, it was she who offered to set up

Chicago is the largest city in the state of Illinois and third-largest city in the United States. Wales lived in this metropolis in the 1990s while working for a company called Chicago Options Associates.

an interview with her boss, Michael Davis.

When Wales walked into Davis's office, Davis had already read his impressive paper on options pricing theory. He was intrigued by the young academic because he happened to need someone who was intelligent and had an eye for business theory to look at his firm's business models and see where things could be improved. He took on the young Wales because he saw a lot of promise in the recent university graduate.

A FUTURE IN FINANCE?

The job that Davis needed Wales for was to go through the firm's current pricing models. Wales enjoyed the change of pace from studying. He also liked seeing after all these

These traders signal the buying and selling of stock options at the Chicago Board Options Exchange. As you can see, it is a very stressful and fast-paced job that Wales ultimately chose to leave behind.

years how the theoretical models that he had studied in college translated to real life. What he learned working under Michael Davis at Chicago Options Associates was that many theories that sounded great on paper didn't work in practice. However, traders working in the marketplace just knew what worked. They could see when existing models were wrong and acted accordingly. Wales learned to develop this sort of intuition, which would come in handy later when he was troubleshooting on the design for Wikipedia.

As much as he enjoyed working on the analytical side of finance, Wales was also eager to try the practical. He decided he wanted to become a trader and learn to make the trades that earned money in the market. Davis described him as a very careful and thorough trader. Wales quickly earned a reputation for being consistently right about his trades—he seldom ever lost money on a deal. However, while this sounds like the makings of a solid trader, Wales's careful approach and consistent accuracy weren't considered unquestionable virtues in the trading world. In options trading, making money on every deal isn't nearly as important as how much money you make on each deal. Davis said of Wales that he could have made much more money on each trade but didn't because he was more interested in being precise. Davis did not believe Wales was aggressive enough to be a career trader. Nevertheless, Wales did well for himself during the early 1990s at Chicago Options Associates. Over time, he was even promoted to become the research director there.

While Wales was triumphing in the finance world, he was also looking into his side interest in computers and computer programming. By day, he worked as research director of Chicago Options Associates and by night he worked on his computer and programming skills. Wales claims that at this point in his life he was completely wrapped up in his work and had no social life.

However, despite Wales's claims that he was too busy for fun, he did manage to get out sometimes. Despite focusing on his career during much of the 1990s, Wales was soon to have a little success in his personal life also. In June 1996, he met Christine Rohan, who was working as a steel trader for the Japanese company Mitsubishi. The two met at a party when a mutual friend arranged for them to talk, hoping they would get along well. As it turns out, the pair got along very well. After a whirlwind summer of dating, during a getaway to Las Vegas, Jimmy proposed to Christine. He hid the engagement ring in the lunch container the airline handed out halfway through the flight. The couple was married in March 1997 in the Florida Keys.

BOMIS: RIDING THE INTERNET WAVE

Around this time, the Internet was really starting to blossom as more and more people were turning to it,

Russian-born author and philosopher Ayn Rand, seen here, wrote a number of books and essays that greatly influenced Wales's thinking and contributed to how he would manage Wikipedia.

and it was becoming easier for users to navigate. While continuing his job at Chicago Options Associates, Wales turned his attention to the Internet in his spare time. Wales was on a mailing list from his university days with another Internet savvy Chicagoan named Tim Shell. Both men were interested in philosophy, particularly in the philosophy of a writer named Ayn Rand called Objectivisim. The two men talked on an online message board about it. It is fitting that they met online because when they met in person, they discovered they had a shared interest in wanting to create a start-up company online. Wales could fund the project with money from his trading job and continue to work on the project with Shell in his spare time.

Before deciding what the company would really do, the men had to settle on a name. From working in the Chicago business world, Wales jokingly referred to them as "bitter old men in suits." The name stuck in the form of an acronym, BOMIS, although officially both men say the name stands for nothing. The company Bomis, Inc. was officially started in 1996, but at the time it didn't have a clear-cut business model. The company went through a number of different business ideas with varying degrees of success.

The first plan for Bomis was to make it a directory for showcasing used cars. Digital cameras were also a

The Philosophy of Objectivism

Wales has always been a fan of the writings and philosophy of Ayn Rand. Ayn Rand was a mid-twentieth-century Russian writer who created the philosophy of Objectivism. Wales first encountered Rand's work when he read one of her novels, *The Fountainhead*, while an undergraduate at the University of Alabama.

The principles of Objectivism appealed to him and can later be seen in his concept for Wikipedia. Essentially, Objectivism is a philosophy that holds that there is a reality that exists independently of how people perceive it. Further, human beings have the power to understand this reality through their senses and can therefore obtain objective knowledge. How does this pertain to Wikipedia? An encyclopedia is intended to be a work of facts: truth free from bias. An entry about panda bears cannot be written by someone who loves pandas any more than it can be written by someone who hates them. It needs to be written objectively and state just the facts about what pandas are, where the live, and how they live their lives. Consider that for an openly edited encyclopedia to work, there must be one reality that they are all working toward despite their different viewpoints and experiences.

If Wales did not believe objective reality was possible, he would not have set out to found Wikipedia.

Interestingly, Ayn Rand's influence on Wales can be seen in more than just his life's work. He also named his daughter, Kira, after the main character in one of Rand's novels, *We the Living*.

very new technology at the time, and Wales and Shell acquired one so they could take and instantly upload photos of used cars from dealerships around the Chicago area. Their hope was to make it easier for people looking for a used car because they could come to one place to get all of the necessary information instead of driving all over town to see what was available. The car dealerships in turn could pay Bomis for the service of showcasing their vehicles. However, Wales and Shell quickly abandoned this idea. Although the start-up costs were low, the investment took a huge amount of legwork to go around taking the pictures and listing the cars. Wales was still working a full-time job at Chicago Options Associates at the time and wanted a project that would make money but still be hands off.

The second idea for Bomis was to make it an online food ordering service. People who wanted to order food for take-out or delivery could go to the Web site and find a number of restaurants to order from without having to pick up a phone. This seemed like a good idea; however, it would require a lot of advertising to get people to come to the service. Otherwise, most people wouldn't know about it and would just continue to look up restaurants in the phone book and call to make orders. Wales and Shell realized they didn't have enough money to invest in Bomis to cover the cost of advertising, so they nixed this business idea, too.

Wales realized they were being too specific with their ideas for Bomis. It needed to have a general usefulness that would suit a number of needs not just for people who were hungry or in the market for cars. The next incarnation of Bomis was a directory of different businesses around Chicago. By attracting repeat visitors to the site, it could make money off of advertising. Once local businesses knew a lot of people were going to the site, they would be willing to pay more to get their ads prominently featured there. Soon Bomis was generating some revenue, and Wales started to look beyond Chicago. He helped expand the site to include all of the United States.

As Bomis expanded outside of Chicago, Wales realized he was ready to move beyond the city, too. By 1998, Bomis

Wales is seen here with his then wife Christine at a *TIME* magazine event honoring him. Christine and Jimmy met while they were both living and working in Chicago.

was generating enough income that Wales could leave his job at Chicago Options Associates, and he decided to move away from Chicago as well. Wales and Shell decided they could run the business just as well from the warmer climate of California. By the end of 1998, Wales and his wife, Christine, had relocated to their new home in San Diego, California.

Bomis grew in the years that followed and soon had as many as eight employees. It was similar to a number of other directories during the early dot-com boom, and while it wasn't the largest, it was known for a number of unique innovations. One of these was the concept of the "ring." This was a way to help people keep ideas together and find new and interesting Web sites on topics they were interested in. People could create rings about many different topics. For example, someone might go to a ring about science on Bomis and when they finished looking at one Web site about some aspect of science, they could visit the next Web site in the ring. It may be hard to believe that this was the easiest way to find new information and Web sites, but in the early days of the Internet boom, there was a great deal of information but no easy way to find any of it. Bomis, along with a number of other search engines, made finding information simpler and more efficient.

Rings were available for many different topics, including topics of particular interest to Wales. Bomis hosted a Web site supporting the Objectivist philosophy that Wales followed. In addition, some of his political views were recognized on a Web site that Bomis hosted called Freedom's Nest. This included a database of books and quotes and an Objectivist Web site that is no longer operating. It was called We the Living after one of Ayn Rand's novels—the same novel that would later lend its name to Wales's only daughter.

CHAPTER 3

The Foundations of Wikipedia

As Bomis became a more profitable enterprise, Wales finally had the money he needed to start a new, slightly riskier project under the Bomis umbrella. For a while, Wales had been thinking about trying to create an online encyclopedia that was different from any subscription-based online encyclopedia where people had to pay a fee to see articles. He wanted to make an encyclopedia where the information was free and available to anyone just by going on the Internet. In order for this to be feasible, part of his idea was that all of the articles would be written by volunteers—scholars and experts on different topics who were willing to donate their knowledge and expertise free of charge. Thanks to the financial success of Bomis, Wales finally had the chance to focus on this idea and create something new and different. He began thinking about how to create and launch such a project in late 1999. He decided to call the project Nupedia.

Richard Stallman has a very impressive résumé—he studied at Harvard and worked at MIT's Artificial Intelligence Lab. In 1984, he resigned from MIT to start the GNU project that would pave the way for Wikipedia.

LICENSE FOR FREE

The name "Nupedia" came from a combination of the word "encyclopedia" and something called the GNU Public License. The GNU Public License was an idea formed largely by a computer programmer named Richard Stallman. He shared many of Wales's ideas that information should be free and open to all people. Stallman had noticed a curious conundrum about information shared over the Internet. Information that was made public domain meant that it was free and could be used by anyone, but there was a catch. Because it was free and could be used by anyone, that meant that users could take it and make changes without sharing these changes. Stallman believed that taking information or programming code and giving nothing back halted overall progress.

He created the GNU Public License through his organization called the Free Software Foundation in order to solve this problem. This license, which is often referred to simply as GNU or GPL, is very simple. It basically states that if you use materials under the GNU license to make something new, then the thing that you create must be under the same license if you want to distribute it.

Let's consider an example. Say you want to use a photo you find online of a man on a surfboard that is under the GNU license. You can use the photo for free and even make changes if you want, like using a computer program to make the surfer's hair brown so that he looks like you. However, when you put this new photo online to show all of your friends and wish them a happy summer, it must be under the GNU license as well. So if others want to take your updated photo and make changes to it and distribute it on their own, they are free to do that.

Nupedia was not the first site supporting volunteer content that would follow and pay homage to GNU. Before Nupedia, in 1998, there was a site called Gnuhoo, that would later evolve into a project called DMOZ. The idea behind DMOZ was to create a directory of Internet sites known as an open source directory. The founders of DMOZ believed that volunteers would participate not to benefit a single company or to make anyone money but because they would be benefiting the public and providing a useful service. Their belief was that by making information free and available to more people, progress would happen more rapidly. Sound familiar? Wikipedia would follow a similar philosophy and goal just ten years later.

Wales first encountered Stallman's work as an early Internet user. In fact, he came across it while he was still in graduate school. He was doing data analysis and came across Stallman's theories on free licensing. At first, Wales wasn't sure what to make of it and thought it was a strange idea. However, time would transform him from a skeptic to a champion of Stallman's ideas. He would go on to use the idea of free information and open content sharing in Nupedia and, ultimately, Wikipedia.

A NEW PARTNER

Wales had met his friend and business partner Tim Shell through an online philosophy mailing list, and among members of this community, he found his newest friend and business partner in Larry Sanger. Sanger was actually a Ph.D. student in philosophy who was very involved with the Internet and programming. Sanger was important in the months leading up to the year 2000 as a creator of a Web site on issues relating to Y2K. Y2K was the concern that at the start of the year 2000, huge problems would be caused because computers wouldn't be able to commute a year not beginning in "19." Luckily, Y2K turned out to be a nonevent and no catastrophe happened. Unluckily for Sanger, it meant he needed a new project.

Shortly after New Year's in 2000, Sanger e-mailed a group of his mailing list connections, including Jimmy Wales, asking if anyone wanted to join him on a new blog project. Wales e-mailed him back. He wasn't interested in a blog, but he had another idea he wanted to try: a free encyclopedia.

Larry Sanger is a former professor of philosophy who was instrumental in helping Wales found Wikipedia. He later created a Web site called Citizendium, which is an alternative to Wikipedia.

Sanger was intrigued by the project, especially when Wales told him that he wanted a philosopher to run the whole thing.

Wales's original idea for the project was to have it be a collaborative work that would use volunteer contributors from all over the Internet. The sources for all the information would be open to anyone so that any reader could see where the information came from. Wales's hope was that although he wouldn't charge for content, the enterprise would still make money for Bomis in the same way that its previous sites had: through the selling of advertising. All the encyclopedia had to do was provide a free service and people would flock to it. Once people started using it, advertisers would jump at the chance to show ads to this new audience.

After finishing his Ph.D., Sanger moved out to San Diego to join Wales and the Bomis team. He became the new editor in chief of Wales's vision, which would soon evolve into Nupedia. Wales wanted his encyclopedia to follow the same basic model as the GNU Public License and so he created the Nupedia Open Content License. While the Nupedia Open Content License was similar to the GNU license, it was not exactly the same. The creator of GNU, Richard Stallman, convinced Wales to switch over to a license called the GNU Free Documentation License. This license is very similar to the GNU Public License, which was designed especially for reference works, including manuals, textbooks, and encyclopedias.

THE PROCESS OF PRODUCING CONTENT

So how do you go about creating an encyclopedia run by volunteers? The first decision that Wales and Sanger had to make was how to deal with the problem of bias. By welcoming volunteers, the encyclopedia would be encouraging a variety of viewpoints and opinions. The encyclopedia would have to find a way to make sure all of these differing points of views came together.

Because of Sanger's academic background, he wanted to make sure that the educational integrity of the encyclopedia was maintained. He wanted to make sure that all of the volunteer contributors were experts in their field. Sanger went to great lengths to make sure that his writers were qualified, including having them fax him their degrees! While Nupedia was a volunteer-run site and anyone could apply to be a writer, all articles were subject to review before approval. Sanger had a lengthy editorial process that involved seven full steps to completing an article, from assignment to finished product. This entire process produced high-quality, well-researched material, but each article could take weeks at a time to produce. In September 2000, the very first article to grace Nupedia was born.

Freeing the Written Word

Wales was not the first to create an open content database dedicated to making information free for everyone. Nor was he the first to harness the power of volunteers to do it. Before the Internet even began, back in 1971, a man named Michael Hart set out to make written works from political documents to classic works of literature available to the masses in a digital format. Beginning with digitizing the United States Declaration of Independence, he stated that his goal was to make the ten thousand most consulted books available to the public for free. He hoped to achieve this goal at the end of the twentieth century. He called the undertaking Project Gutenberg after Johannes Gutenberg, who revolutionized the spread of information and the written word by creating the printing press.

Even before the Internet, and in the early 1970s, Hart believed that computers would take off and that having books in a digital format would be a way to make sure they could be seen by everyone. His Project Gutenberg has more than succeeded in its goal, largely through the work of volunteers. In 1989, the software that Project Gutenberg used to scan books into computer text was imperfect. Smudges on the page or dust could cause errors.

Volunteers offered to proofread the scanned text to fix these errors, so that the works of literature were kept in their original condition. The result was the perfect model of volunteers and computers working together to create a free online database for the masses. It was a model Wales would hope to emulate twenty years later with his own information-sharing project, Nupedia.

Project Gutenberg's founder Michael Hart died in September 2011 but not before seeing his vision realized. Today, Project Gutenberg has around thirty-six thousand e-books in its collection with up to fifty new e-books added every day.

It was called "atonality," and it was about a specific aspect of music theory. The author was a German music scholar, and the completed article was only a page, but it contained many footnotes and almost thirty references. Overall, the author of this first article set the bar very high for future articles.

Sanger and Wales soon noticed a problem with Nupedia's rigorous procedures. The problem was that despite the high-quality material produced, it simply took too long for a single article to be finished. In the first year that Nupedia was up and running, it produced fewer than fifty articles. This was hardly the information-rich encyclope-dia that Wales had initially envisioned. However, Wales didn't fully realize the problem and the reason that Nupe-dia was failing to gather a mass of writers and articles until he attempted to write an article himself. To make use of his several half-finished graduate degrees in busi-ness and his years at Chicago Options Associates, Wales chose to write about options pricing theory just like his published paper many years before. It seemed an easy enough task given his background, and yet Wales found that under the strict editorial process set up by Sanger, the writing was tedious, and it felt like homework. If one of the founders of a project couldn't enjoy writing an article, how could they expect an army of volunteers to willingly offer their services? Wales saw the need for a complete overhaul of Nupedia.

At the end of 2000 and Nupedia's first full year, Sanger and Wales were at a standstill. They knew something desperately had to change to make Nupedia the robust resource that Wales had hoped to create, but they had no idea how to go about doing it. It would be only one month later that they would transform Nupedia into a Web site that would change the world: Wikipedia.

CHAPTER 4

Wikipedia Rises

So how did Wales help to raise Wikipedia from the ashes of the failed venture Nupedia? The pieces began to fall into place when Wales heard from a fellow Bomis employee named Jeremy Rosenfeld about something that might be the answer to their problems with Nupedia. It was a Web site called WikiWikiWeb. The word "wiki" is a Hawaiian word meaning "quick," and "wiki wiki" means "super quick." It was a fitting name for the site because it could be updated at a very rapid rate. This Web site was special in that, using no complicated software, it made it possible for anyone to edit the page. WikiWikiWeb encouraged ultimate collaboration as anyone could add to or change something on the page even if that person was in a completely different part of the world.

This might not seem like a huge advance, but at the time it represented something truly unique. At this time, editing Web pages was not as easy for the average person as it is today. People were not used to updating blogs, writing tweets, or creating their own personal sites. In order

The main page of Wikipedia's English edition, known as "the Free Encyclopedia," offers readers a chance to read a featured article of the day or browse entries at random.

to edit a Web page in the year 2000, you had to have a knowledge of computer code. It was a complex process that very few people on the Internet ever attempted. However, WikiWikiWeb changed all of that. All people had to do was click a button that said "edit" and they could change anything they wanted. Not only that, but these changes immediately went live on the site.

It is worth noting that there is some controversy and disagreement between Jimmy Wales and Larry Sanger on who actually discovered the wiki concept. Sanger maintains that before Jeremy Rosenfeld told Wales about it, Sanger himself heard of the site from a longtime friend named Ben Kovitz, who was a computer programmer. However,

Wikipedia,
that anyone can edit.
les in English

rticle

Lenz vector is a vector
nomical body around a
by Newtonian gravity, th
r where it is calculated

Interpedia: The Encyclopedia That Wasn't

Although Wikipedia was a unique Web site that changed the way we research information online, there were a number of sites that helped pave the way for Wikipedia's success. So was Nupedia a unique concept in early Internet history? There was actually another idea for an Internet encyclopedia that predated Wikipedia and even Nupedia.

In 1993, a man named Richard Gates saw that the Internet could be used to reach out to a number of experts in different fields. He hoped that they could pool their knowledge and publish a number of articles in one place in an Internet encyclopedia called Interpedia. A number of people got behind the idea, including Mike Hart, the founder of Project Gutenberg. For about six months, Richard Gates and other interested parties discussed the idea for Interpedia on message boards and tried to fine-tune the idea. However, ironically, it is perhaps because of the extreme growth of the World Wide Web around this time that the members lost interest and moved on to other projects. The idea fizzled out before it had a chance to be realized.

However, the idea for Interpedia is an interesting one because it relied on a system of "seals of approval." The group could vote on all of the articles so that each article would either receive a seal of approval or not. No article would be rejected, but those without a seal of approval would naturally fall into disuse. Wales would implement a similar method of vetting articles on his own Internet encyclopedia, Wikipedia, by surveying readers on an article's correctness.

regardless of how the knowledge came to the Nupedia creators, it was neither Ben Kovitz nor Jereremy Rosenfeld who was actually the creator of WikiWikiWeb. The real man behind WikiWikiWeb was Ward Cunningham, who had spent nearly ten years developing the site. An important aspect of Ward's creation was that even though anyone could change a page on it, every single version of every page was saved forever. This meant that people didn't have to worry about causing lasting damage if they got something wrong. If someone changed something that shouldn't be changed, the page could always be reverted to an older version. A community began to form around the site as contributors adopted what they called "wiki culture."

WIKIWIKIWEB BECOMES WIKIPEDIA

Wales could immediately see the potential in using Wiki-WikiWeb to jump-start Nupedia's sluggish performance of the last year. Both he and Sanger were hopeful that Ward Cunningham's design would help solve the problem of long editorial processes and turn the trickle of articles into a flood. While there was some disagreement between Wales and Sanger over who discovered Wiki and thought it would be a good idea for Nupedia, they both agree it was Sanger who chose the name for the new creation: Wikipedia. Originally, the creators of Nupedia thought that Wiki would be a separate project that would merely generate content that they could then pluck once it had blossomed and put it on Nupedia. It was only a week into the undertaking that they realized Nupedia wasn't the future—Wikipedia was. Of all of the Nupedia articles that made it through the editorial process, only two did so after 2001. Meanwhile, the Wikipedia site was launched as its own project under Wikipedia.com on January 15, 2001. What was the very first article to grace the informational Web page? It was about the history and origins of the letter "U."

Almost within its first week, a community was already forming around Wikipedia. A handful of Nupedia's volunteers started writing articles, and through advertising over mailing lists and in forums, the word begin to spread. In its first few weeks of operation, Wikipedia had nearly five thousand people access it. By the end of its first month, Wikipedia had six hundred articles in total. That's ten times more than Nupedia had created in its first year. Part of the success of Wikipedia was due to a Web site called Slashdot.org. This site was a meeting place for computer-savvy and technically knowledgeable people in the computer community. It was a site where tech-savvy people could pick up the latest news and information and also produce it. Similar to the users of Wikipedia, the users of Slashdot formed a community and helped sift through each other's work. The editors of Slashdot wrote an article on the launch of Wikipedia in early 2001. This introduced the Slashdot community to a new place where they could share information. Many of the Slashdot readers decided to become Wikipedia editors, creating a wave of new articles for the young site.

However, even in light of Wikipedia's near immediate success, there were still a few issues that needed to be worked out. As Ward Cunningham had originally envisioned it, Wiki was more of a notepad, giving collaborators a chance to share ideas and build on each other's works. However, for a work like an encyclopedia that is a finished product that people are supposed to see as fact, having a bunch of different people's notes all over it made the site confusing. Luckily, the person who had made the original code for Wikipedia was eager to offer his services to fix this issue. From the programmers at work troubleshooting on the site to the army of writers and editors producing content, a community of willing volunteers was already at work.

THE EVOLUTION OF WIKIPEDIA

Wikipedia has evolved over its ten plus years of existence, and Wales has continued to help shape and define that evolution. By the end of its first year, the site had expanded into eighteen different languages thanks to its network of international volunteers. Toward the end of 2002, the Web site had twenty-six different language editions, which would balloon to over forty by the end of 2004. Meanwhile Nupedia's days were numbered. Nupedia coexisted with Wikipedia after its initial launch, but by the end of 2003, Nupedia's servers

were shut down, and its limited content was absorbed by Wikipedia. By 2007, the English version of Wikipedia had

After being dissuaded by the housing market, Wales moved from San Diego to St. Petersburg, Florida, seen here, in 2002. He currently resides in this coastal city, which is a popular tourist destination.

a whopping two million articles. At this point it eclipsed any other encyclopedia in existence for sheer quantity of articles. This included passing the *Yongle Encyclopedia*, which was a work of over two thousand Chinese scholars under the direction of the Yongle Emperor in China in the 1400s. Before Wikipedia, the *Yongle Encyclopedia* had held the record for largest collection of information for an astounding six hundred years.

Up until late 2002, Wikipedia.com was still a for-profit business under the umbrella of Bomis. However, Wales soon decided that Wikipedia would ultimately be a better resource if it wasn't affected by advertising. He decided to move the site to Wikipedia.org and make it a

nonprofit organization. A possible motive for the move was the fact that the Spanish edition of Wikipedia had

Sue Gardner is the current executive director of the Wikimedia Foundation. She took over the position in December of 2007 and has seen the foundation grow and change, including moving its headquarters from Florida to California.

branched off in February of that year complaining that it didn't like the fact that the Web site had advertising on it. The Spanish sect created another site called the Enciclopedia Libre, which is Spanish for "free encyclopedia." As an interesting side note, after the Enciclopedia Libre was formed, the old Spanish version of Wikipedia suffered for lack of content for some time. However, around June 2003, as the popularity of Wikipedia in general began to soar, Spanish Wikipedia began to bounce back. Editors took on the project, and many were completely unaware of the history of Spanish Wikipedia. It would reach more than ten thousand articles by the end of 2003 alone, and in the fall of 2004, Spanish Wikipedia would eclipse Enciclopedia Libre in number of articles.

After Wikipedia made the switch from .com to .org, it was no longer controlled by Bomis but rather was hosted and funded by a new nonprofit called the Wikimedia Foundation. The Wikimedia Foundation has a number of local chapters that help raise funding for the organization. Jimmy Wales is the chairman emeritus, essentially an honorary title, of the board of trustees for the Wikimedia Foundation and has been since he founded it. The organization has its headquarters in St. Petersburg, Florida, where Wales had moved from San Diego in 2002.

The Wikimedia Foundation is an umbrella for a number of open source sites similar to Wikipedia. These include Wikimedia Commons, which shares many photos and images that are free to use either because they are in the public domain or because the artists themselves have posted them under the Wikimedia free license. Also, there is Wiktionary, an open source dictionary. There is also Wikiversity, which offers teaching tools and help to students, including easy-to-follow information and helpful charts and images. There is also a news site called Wikinews, which provides fast coverage of current events.

The Wikimedia Foundation holds twice-a-year fundraisers to get money for these different sites under its umbrella. Despite being mostly volunteer-run in terms of content, there are still some costs associated with maintaining the sites. In order to keep Wikipedia and the other Wikimedia Foundation sites free for all and free of advertising, these periodic fund-raisers are necessary. The community that flocks to offer their time and knowledge to Wikipedia is also apparently willing to open their wallets to give to this cause. Many of the Wikimedia Foundation's fund-raisers take in hundreds of thousands of dollars—and most of these donations come from everyday people, $20 at a time.

In 2008, the headquarters of the Wikimedia Foundation moved from St. Petersburg, Florida, to San Francisco, California. Wales did not move to San Francisco with the organization but maintained a "community founder" seat on the foundation's board of directors.

CHAPTER 5

Wikipedia and the Future of Research

As Jimmy Wales's lasting legacy, Wikipedia has single-handedly changed the way people access information online. It has changed the way people do research, try to gain a general understanding of almost any topic, and look up information on pop culture or current events seemingly minutes after they've happened. When creating Wikipedia, Jimmy Wales asked people to imagine a world where the sum of all human knowledge is available for free to anyone who can access the Internet. This is the kind of world that he was hoping to achieve by founding Wikipedia.

In a lot of ways, it seems as though Wales's vision has come true. It is hard to search for anything on the Internet without Wikipedia coming up within the top five options and very often as the number one result. The scope of the project is absolutely enormous. Wikipedia contains well over a billion words. That's several times larger than the two largest pay-per-use online encyclopedias—Britannica and Encarta—combined. Wikipedia has the largest number of articles in English—to the tune of more than 3.5 million articles, but this is only a fraction of its total number. Wikipedia is made up of articles in other languages, making it a truly global project. There are more than one million articles in German alone and another million in French. In fact, there are almost 40 different languages that have more than 100,000 articles. Across all of Wikipedia, there are nearly 20 million articles with editions in over 280 languages. And these numbers are growing all the time.

But while Wikipedia provides a great number of articles, it is equally important to consider who is accessing this free service. For a site to make information truly available to the masses, the masses must be aware of and see the value of the undertaking. So how popular is Wikipedia really? According to Alexa, which is a Web information company that reports how much traffic Web sites get, Wikipedia is seventh in overall Internet traffic for all Web sites in the world. More people turn to Wikipedia for online news than to any other news source. This means that Wikipedia now has a broader reach than the sites for the *New York Times*, the *Wall Street Journal*, the *Los Angeles Times*, or the *Chicago Tribune*. In fact, Wikipedia has more unique visitors per day than the Web sites of all of these top newspapers combined.

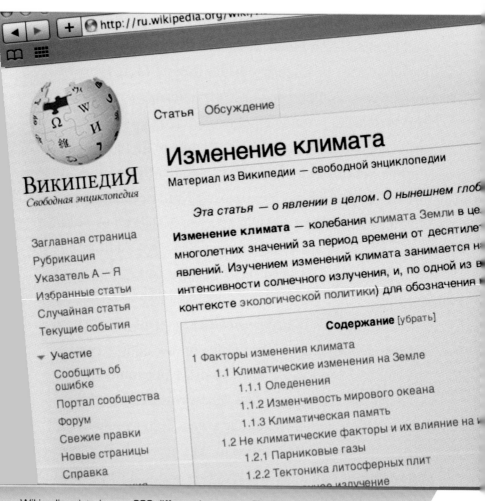

Wikipedia exists in over 280 different languages. The Russian version of the site, seen here, was founded in 2001 and today has over 800,000 articles.

THE RULES OF WIKIPEDIA

Early on in the development of Wikipedia, Wales and Sanger planned out what they thought the core rules and

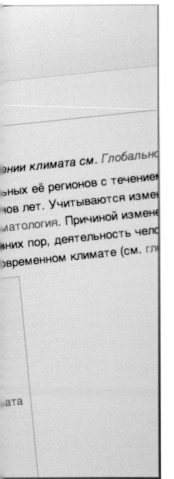

нии климата см. Глобальн

ьных её регионов с течением

юв лет. Учитываются измен

матология. Причиной измене

них пор, деятельность чело

временном климате (см. гл

ата

guidelines of Wikipedia should be. The biggest one that they thought Wikipedia needed to have was a neutral point of view, or NPOV. According to Wales, NPOV is the only completely nonnegotiable guideline of Wikipedia's three main policies. The other two policies that Wikipedia maintains is that all work has to be verified by another source and that no original research can be published. These two policies essentially amount to the same thing: you can't present facts without backing them up with another source. Even if you have personally done research and seen something firsthand, you can't present that information for the first time in Wikipedia. It needs to be in a scholarly journal, newspaper, or other verifiable source.

This means that you can't just go on Wikipedia and write anything you believe because only through verifiable fact can a neutral point of view be maintained. Let's say you believe that a species called the strawberry frog lives only in the rain forest of South America. You could not make an article about the strawberry frog unless you could point to an article in another source detailing the habitat of the amphibian. This would be true even if you were a trusted biologist who had been studying the strawberry frog and had personally seen one hop across your hand while in the rain forests of South America. The only way you could create an article on Wikipedia about your findings is if they had been published in a trusted scientific publication that you could reference.

In addition to the three main policies outlined above, Wikipedia has over time honed a list of five unchanging pillars that reflect both it rules and its missions. The five pillars state that (1) Wikipedia is an encyclopedia, (2) Wikipedia has a neutral point of view, (3) Wikipedia is free content, (4) Wikipedia has a code of conduct, and (5) Wikipedia does not have firm rules. These five pillars effectively summarize what Wikipedia is and why it works so well. Wales believes that people will behave without strict rules telling them what to do. All they need is a firm mission and the freedom to play around a little, and they will form a community.

THE SUCCESS OF THE WIKIPEDIA COMMUNITY

How does a community begin to form? People are inherently social animals who naturally form communities. Throughout human history we have hunted together and grown food to survive. We have the desire to reach out to other people and to work toward common goals. It is these

Irish sociology student Shane Fitzgerald tried to test the reliability of Wikipedia's community by intentionally submitting a fake quote in 2009. The Wikipedia community noticed the quote wasn't properly attributed and removed it.

factors of human existence that help make Wikipedia possible. The Wikipedia community works without a lot of direction from Jimmy Wales. He set up the system, and people use it effortlessly.

Wales is the first to admit that he is not the only one responsible for the success of Wikipedia. The success of this enterprise rests firmly on the strength of the community behind it. As Wales explains, the idea behind Wikipedia was not necessarily a technological one—the Internet and components necessary had been around a number of years before its founding. Rather the creation of Wikipedia with its open source database and theory of free information is a social advancement. For the Web site to be successful a group of people had to be willing to give their time and knowledge to the world for free. Not only that, but they had to care about the project enough to vet other articles and make sure the information going online was as accurate as possible. There is a joke about Wikipedia that it is something that works only in practice, but not in theory. In practice, the information juggernaut exceeds expectations. People would assume that an encyclopedia that anyone could edit would turn into an impossible to understand mess of differing viewpoints. However, Wikipedia has a strong group of volunteers who police it for incorrect information and who are committed to constantly improving it.

Wales believes that the reason the Wikipedia community is so strong is because he puts so much faith in them. Because all of the information is under the free license discussed in chapter 3, people are more willing to donate their writing and knowledge because they know it is going toward the community. The terms and conditions of Wikipedia are much more basic than for most Web sites—Wikipedia doesn't spend a lot of time restricting what people can do or how they can use the information they find on the site.

An example Wales gave in the foreword he wrote for the book *The Wikipedia Revolution* is that he compares how he planned Wikipedia to how a restaurant might plan its design. If the restaurant was planning to serve steak, it would realize it needed to provide steak knives. Steak knives are sharp enough to cut through tough meat, but the downside is they might also be used by people as weapons. However, rather than plan for this by putting people who order steak in cages to protect them from each other, restaurants count on the fact that social norms will keep the vast majority of people from arming themselves with cutlery and starting a brawl. Wales believes that many Web sites write their terms and conditions by thinking of all of the bad things people might do and then setting up barriers to keep them from happening. With Wikipedia, Wales proves that given a little freedom, most people will

Wikipedia Culture

Imagine yourself at a youth hostel in Germany surrounded by writers, students, and computer programmers from around the world all there for one reason: Wikipedia. In August 2005, this was a reality, as one of the first Wikipedia conferences was held. Many of the hundreds of people who gathered had never met each other, and many knew each other merely by screen names, but despite all of this, they had been working together toward a common goal for years. That goal was creating Wikipedia, an encyclopedia for the masses.

This very diverse group of people from different backgrounds who hailed from all over the world begin to form a culture as they took on a name: Wikipedians. They called this early conference where they joined together in real life to share their common triumphs a Wikimania conference. These users had all put forth their talents for free and for no purpose greater than to combine knowledge together and make a reliable resource. It was the community that Wales had envisioned and put his faith in. These men and women were happy to do what they did merely to celebrate their success, four years after Wikipedia had been launched, and to meet their cocollaborators for the first time.

At the time of this first Wikimania conference in Germany, Wikipedia had already become one of the top fifty Web sites in the world, and in just a few months more, it would be in the top thirty. These volunteers had a lot to celebrate: their success, Wales's success, and the success of Wikipedia.

not try to dismantle the system and will follow the rules as set out. Of course, there will always be a few people who try to intentionally put misinformation online or otherwise disrupt the process. However, thanks to Wikipedia's strong community, these errors are almost instantly fixed.

Although Wales was not the first to coin the phrase, he is a fan of the term "piranha effect" to describe the power of the Wikipedia community. A piranha is a small, meat-eating Amazonian fish that travels in large groups and has razor sharp teeth. When one piranha bites its prey it doesn't do that much, but a feeding frenzy of piranhas can devour an entire cow. The carnivorous swimmers act as a single unit toward a common goal. They naturally group together, with each one attracted to the activities of the others. Wales explains in interviews that the same thing happens with members of the Wikipedia community.

They start with an article that isn't perfect, and sometimes not even very good, and then they pick at it and pick at it until they form a feeding frenzy of edits that ends with not a bad article at all.

As Wikipedia evolved, Wales and his team started looking for ways they could use the community to make Wikipedia better and better. One of these methods was in finding ways to trigger the piranha effect and signal people when articles could use a little work. Most articles start out as incomplete "stubs." These stubs are just a fragment of what the article will grow into with a little care from the Wikipedia community. A normal encyclopedia, newspaper, or other source of information would never leave a first draft up for everyone to see at its worst. However, in the Wikipedia community, putting up a first draft is the same as putting up an invitation for someone in the community to polish it. A stub is a signal that something needs work and that more editors need to give it some attention. As Wikipedia evolved, Wales and the team found that they could further draw people in by labeling stubs and putting them in a category of all stubs. When people wanted to get involved and help the project, they could go directly to a page of articles that needed the most work. To ensure that people would know a stub when they came across it, these incomplete, new articles had the following written at the top of the page: "This article is a stub. You can help Wikipedia by expanding it."

Wikipedia seemed to grow and balloon without stopping for the first several years of its creation. However, around 2007, the growth that had seemed endless suddenly stalled. The English language version was no longer gaining new articles at the same clip. Whereas previously it has been doubling in size each year, in this year the growth curve rounded off and could no longer be described by anyone as explosive or exponential. This is not to say that Wikipedia wasn't still a robust and growing resource with, at the time, around two million articles. Rather the novelty seemed to be wearing off, and some of Wikipedia's loyal community was producing less. While the ebb and flow of articles produced changes throughout the years, the sheer volume of articles that the Web site has achieved is astounding.

Certain members of the volunteer community graduated from being just normal everyday volunteers to becoming site administrators. Admins of Wikipedia have special responsibilities and privileges. For example, Wikipedia admins can update the main landing page, which not everyone can edit because it is susceptible to vandals. Also, Wikipedia admins could choose to block users that they felt were not obeying the rules. In Wikipedia's early days, anyone who wanted to could be an admin. Wales wanted to keep Wikipedia informal, so the process for becoming an admin was simply to ask. Unless there was a reason not to trust someone, the person was almost immediately granted admin privileges. Often these decisions would happen by consensus over e-mail. However, by 2003, as Wikipedia grew bigger and more complex, this was no longer possible. People who came across the site and wanted to be admins now had to apply on Wikipedia.

TROLLS AND VANDALS: DEALING WITH THE DOWNSIDES OF AN OPEN SOURCE COMMUNITY

Despite Wikipedia's strong community feeling, in any group there are always a few bad apples. On Wikipedia, these took the form of trolls. These are not the type of trolls that hide under bridges in fairy tales. In Internet speak, a troll is a person who intentionally causes trouble. Trolls are fairly easy troublemakers to deal with because they are simple to pick out as people who have no interest in adding anything to the community. Their posts are flagged, and these users can eventually be blocked from posting on Wikipedia. There are a host of other vandals on Wikipedia who make bad edits with varying degrees of negative intent. Some of these vandals don't really mean to damage the site but are simply testing out their power. These people can't believe that the Web site would really allow anyone to edit it, so they try their hand at it.

Wikipedia wishes no ill will toward this particular type of vandal. In fact, while undoing these users' test edits, the Wikipedia Web site would often send them a welcome message from the site. This was a way not only to show the new users that their edits were noticed and already fixed but also hopefully to transform them from vandals to useful contributors to the site.

There is unfortunately a more malicious breed of vandals who simply want to post misinformation for the sake of damaging the overall encyclopedia. These pranksters are harder to deal with and less likely to turn around and become welcome volunteers. So how does Wikipedia keep vandals from overrunning the site? The key is fixing all errors quickly and as soon as they are noticed. To aid this, the Web site created something called the Recent Changes page. The Recent Changes page shows a log of every change in the system. A group of volunteers who call themselves the Recent Change Patrol continuously checks this page for updates that might not be correct. Some vandals will make very obvious, incorrect edits, such as inserting profanity into articles. Other vandals are more subtle and will make harder to discern changes, like transposing the numbers in a date.

During the first four years that Wikipedia was up and running the Recent Change Patrol was enough to keep vandals' edits from taking over the site. However, around 2005, the sheer volume of edits made it impossible for even a dedicated army of volunteers to keep up with them all. As times changed and Wikipedia grew, the patrol to prevent vandalism had to adapt. Their response was to add computer programs or bots that could help eliminate some of the more obvious vandals. These sophisticated bots are programmed to recognize certain words or phrases that are telltale signs of vandalism. They also flag users who are more likely to vandalize based on past experience. Volunteers help the bots become more accurate by tweaking their returns from time to time. In chapter 3, you learned about the perfect marriage of computer technology tweaked by human intelligence used in the Gutenberg Project. The process used by the new evolving Recent Changes Patrol was a similar balance. It is not a perfect system, but it allows Wikipedia to stay a couple of steps ahead of the vandals.

FIX IT YOURSELF

Although it doesn't happen as much now given the extreme popularity of Wikipedia, there are still users who occasionally stumble on Wikipedia unaware of its origins or the possibilities for errors. After all, to the uninitiated, how can something that calls itself an encyclopedia possibly have errors? It can still be a shock to these users who have not yet fully digested the idea of completely user-generated content. For these confused newcomers, Wikipedians have adopted a policy that is something of a mantra: SOFIXIT. Basically, this short motto can be a response to any queries or complaints from new users and even sometimes to Wikipedia's critics. It is the answer to nearly every question. Did you notice that the date on an article on World War II battles is wrong? Fix it yourself. Did you find that there is a typo on the third line of an article on Impressionist painting? Fix it yourself. Know of a better way to display an image or organize an article's layout? Fix it yourself.

Because of Wikipedia's editing model, the very people who complain about inaccuracies have the power to change them. Many of these new users in the early days of Wikipedia were not even aware they had this power and would send Wikipedia the corrections they saw just as they would about an error in a newspaper article or book. The administrators of Wikipedia soon created a reply to send back. This reply was intended to welcome the new readers and also to encourage them to try their hand at editing (as they clearly have an eye for noting errors). It was a several sentence message, easily summed up as: See something wrong? Fix it yourself.

Of course, there are downsides to the freedom Wikipedia allows its volunteer editors. One of the limits of Wikipedia is that, by default, any edit to an article becomes available immediately. This happens before any bots can go to work on it or any humans can weed out incorrect information or the Wikipedian feeding frenzy can polish it up. This means that an article may contain some biased contributions, obvious advocacy for a certain cause, the occasional outright error, and sometimes just plain nonsense. These blemishes will remain until another editor comes along to correct the problems. As Wikipedia has spread around the globe into hundreds of different languages, the different language editions have been given the freedom to choose if they would like to continue with the policy or if they would like to make editing a more regulated process.

An example of exercising this freedom can be seen in the German version of Wikipedia. The German version of Wikipedia manages its system through the use of a number of "stable versions" of articles. It allows most readers to see only versions of articles that have passed certain editorial reviews. This method is, in a sense, a combination of the rigorous editorial processes from the time of Nupedia and the laid-back, informal submission structure of Wikipedia. The original Wikipedia—the English language version—uses a similar technique of restriction on some of its more frequently edited articles. Certain high-risk articles are made uneditable to new users to avoid vandalism. These high-risk articles are often on subjects like the biographies of controversial living figures who for political or social reasons are likely to be the subject of biased entries or wrong information. The articles on George W. Bush and Barack Obama fall into this category of protected entries. In an amusing side note, one of these protected entries is actually on elephants. While elephants are not traditionally seen as a hot button topic, the article experienced issues with vandalism. Why were so many people interested in changing the article on elephants? In 2006, the comedian Stephen Colbert, who has a television show on the cable network Comedy Central, suggested to viewers that they go onto Wikipedia and change the elephant article to say that the number of elephants in the world has tripled in the last six months. His viewers listened. The show aired at 11:30 PM EST, and by 11:40 PM EST editors had noticed a flurry of activity and had to shut the article down to edits.

While many of these articles still have locks of some kind on them, Wales is constantly evolving Wikipedia and its policies and looking for ways to have fewer restrictions on users. In June 2010, Wikipedia's administrators announced that the English Wikipedia would remove strict editing restrictions from controversial articles. In place of the old system of making it impossible for new or unregistered users to edit these entries, there would be a new system. Wales called this system "pending changes." He told the BBC that it would make it possible for the largest branch of Wikipedia "to open up articles for general editing that have been protected or semi-protected for years." Introduced on June 15, 2010, the "pending changes" system helped open up all Wikipedia articles for

Comic television host Stephen Colbert played a prank on Wikipedia by asking his viewers to update the article on elephants with false information. To combat the overwhelming response from Colbert's viewers, the article was locked down.

revisions by editors regardless of their standing in the Wikipedia community. Under this new system, edits to specified articles could be made by anyone but are subject to review from an established Wikipedia editor who has shown him- or herself to be reliable and fact-conscious before the article is published. It is similar to the German Wikipedia in some ways, but it allows for a shorter editorial process. Wales chose to opt against the German Wikipedia model because it required an editor to review edits to any article regardless of how frequently it was edited or how hot button a topic. Wales doesn't believe there is a reason to restrict access to all articles, as it goes against one of his main beliefs about the community of Wikipedians that he has fostered.

Wikitorials

In 2005, Wikipedia was already a huge success and well known around the world. Soon, other people were trying to copy the success of the experiment through other mediums outside of Wikipedia. One of these was the *Los Angeles Times*. This newspaper decided to have an editorial column that anyone could edit, just like Wikipedia. However, it would be an editorial rather than an encyclopedia entry, so it was intended to gather opinions rather than facts. The newspaper coined the term "wikitorial" to describe its curious undertaking.

Wales was intrigued by the project and agreed to contribute to the wikitorial idea and see if it could be successful. On June 17, 2005, the *Los Angeles Times* launched the first wikitorial on a very polarizing political subject: the Iraq War. Many Americans had very different opinions about this subject, and many were very forceful in these opinions. The newspaper had chosen a topic that it expected to get very strong opinions about for that very reason. It wanted to really test what a wikitorial could become.

The first wikitorial was launched on June 19, 2005. Amazingly, just two days after the launch, the *Los Angeles Times* was forced to close it. What went wrong in such a short time? The response was overwhelming, but in light of having the ability to frame an opinion and edit an article to express it, people didn't play nearly as nice as they did when trying to agree on facts. The article was repeatedly vandalized, and the newspaper realized that what it was left with was not a publishable article at all. Shortly after 5:00 AM the connection was broken permanently. The wikitorial experiment had failed.

During the two short days the wikitorial was available, it had increased in length from the original eleven thousand words to more than double its size, to become twenty-seven thousand words.

USING WIKIPEDIA FOR RESEARCH

Wikipedia has found many critics among teachers and librarians because many students take information from Wikipedia as fact and even go so far as to cite it in their research papers. So if Wikipedia isn't always factually accurate, does this mean Wales's mission has failed and the site is in fact not a useful source of information? Just because Wikipedia should not be cited in academic work does not mean that it isn't an incredibly useful research

Many students now use Wikipedia to complete assignments for school. Wikipedia can be a useful tool for homework only if the user understands its limitations and facts are double-checked.

tool, so long as it is used correctly and its limitations are understood.

As with any source, you have to question the validity of the facts you read. Just because someone has written them down does not mean that everything is actually correct. However, while you might not want to rely on Wikipedia for specific facts like dates, it is an excellent source for getting a basic understanding of almost any topic. Let's say your teacher assigned you Margaret Mitchell's novel *Gone With the Wind* to read. Using Wikipedia to get a synopsis of the book itself would in no way prepare you for the assignment, but you could use the online resource to get a sense of the context of the novel. You might want to read about the Civil War and life in the plantation-era South to better understand the motivations of the characters in the novel.

In addition, Wikipedia is a good resource for research because many of its sources are cited. Let's say you have an assignment to research and write a paper on the Battle of Gettysburg but aren't sure where to start. You can look up the topic on Wikipedia and scroll down to the external links and source links. Wales was intent on making Wikipedia as accurate as possible by asking that volunteers cite their sources. You can use this list of external links or look up the books mentioned. Of course, you will need to make sure these sources are published by reliable organizations themselves, but it is a good place to start to get a number of online and print resources about a topic.

CHAPTER 6

Jimmy Wales: Wikipedia and Beyond

In mid-December 2001, Wales had the unfortunate task of laying off his friend and business partner Larry Sanger. Despite the extreme success of Wikipedia, as a nonprofit it was no longer making money for Bomis, which was then forced to lay off most of its staff. Sanger was officially laid off at the beginning of February 2002 but stayed around as a volunteer until March. From this point on, Wales became the single face of Wikipedia. His leadership style was very hands-off as he felt he could put a lot of faith in the Wikipedians to run themselves in an orderly fashion. He oversaw the project and stepped in on certain cases, but by and large for the next couple of years, Wikipedia ran like a well-oiled machine.

As we discussed in the previous section, with any community that opens itself to the whole world, there will always be a couple of bad apples who choose to vandalize rather than add useful information. These vandals run the

Wales is seen here in an interview in London in 2011. To keep Wikipedia free for everyone, Wales continues to travel the world to raise money and awareness about the work of the Wikimedia Foundation.

gambit from the malicious person to the bored college student. While many of these issues are taken care of by volunteers, larger disputes often call for a mediator. Wales would weigh in on disputes and issues that arose on a one-on-one basis. While Wikipedia was still relatively small, he was able to give each issue personal attention. He still kept a fairly hands-off approach and would intervene only when expressly asked.

However, as Wikipedia grew in size and scope, Wales was no longer able to take on each individual problem. Additionally, he was increasingly called away to all parts of the globe for press conferences and interviews as interest in his project increased. Wales realized that he no longer had the time to devote to the daily disputes that might arise. Rather than hire someone to replace him as Wikipedia's town sheriff, he again turned to the Wikipedia

Wookieepedia

Many of the wikis hosted on Wikia offer the same sort of information as Wikipedia but in much greater depth than what is found in the general encyclopedia. The average person looking for an article on knitting on Wikipedia would expect a history and perhaps a rundown of basic techniques, but not the level of detail or advice that only a true knitting enthusiast could appreciate and that can be found on the knitting wiki on Wikia.

Some wikis take on a life of their own and become positively enormous and steeped in detail. One of the largest wikis currently on Wikia is Wookieepedia, a site that is active and has more than eighty-six thousand articles devoted to the *Star Wars* series. Wookieepedia was launched on March 4, 2005, on Wikia. By April of that same year, it was the most visited wiki on Wikia. By November, the page had been selected by Syfy Channel as its "Sci Fi Site of the Week."

Although it is the English language Wookieepedia that boasts the largest number of articles, Wikia hosts Star Wars wikis in nearly twenty languages, from Serbian to Japanese. Wookieepedia also coordinates its efforts with the German language wiki called Jedipedia.net and the Polish language Biblioteka

Ossus. There is also the Slovak Darthpedia and the Korean Forcepedia. As a source of news on the movies, a quote of the day, and articles on everything from J8Q Finbat Missiles to minor characters without speaking roles, the force is definitely with this wiki.

community to provide a solution. In November 2004, Wales asked the Wikipedians to create a committee for "Wikiquette," or Wikipedia etiquette. This group would settle small disputes by committee by either mediating between two parties or making a final judgment on what would be done.

Like all people in the public eye, Jimmy Wales has not entirely escaped controversy. In late 2005, Wales came under attack for editing his own biography on Wikipedia, a practice generally frowned on when it came to the biographies of living people. When it came to light that Wales had edited his biography close to twenty times, he was asked to explain. In interviews, Wales said that he was making changes only to correct factual errors as would be done with any evolving article. He added that while it was generally frowned on to edit one's own biography, there was no official rule preventing it. In the end, Wales apologized for making the edits and agreed that it was a good policy to avoid editing one's own biography because it is impossible to be objective about yourself. He knows that it is important to hold himself just as accountable for maintaining the most important of Wikipedia's policies: a neutral point of view. The incident makes clear the sort of power that Wikipedia has. Essentially it is the power to rewrite history. This is something Wales hopes to avoid, as it was never his aim in beginning the project to change facts, only to record them. He is committed to trying to make Wikipedia as factually accurate a resource as possible.

WALES'S POST-WIKIPEDIA PURSUITS

Having been the primary founder of a Web site that has changed the way people research information online, you might think Jimmy Wales would be content to enjoy his success. However, just as in the early days of Bomis, Wales is constantly looking for new and interesting projects that he can work on. He is still very involved with Wikipedia and many of his side projects are very much Wiki related.

Wales is an honorary member of the Berkman Center for Internet & Society at Harvard Law School. His status there is fitting as the mission of this school is to explore and understand cyberspace. Another place where his expertise and insight is valued is on the advisory board of the MIT Center for Collective Intelligence, which focuses on new ways that people are communicating and sharing information through the Internet. Outside of these respected academic institutions, he is on the board of directors at Creative Commons, which is a nonprofit devoted to sharing arts and culture in the same way that Wikipedia shares information. As of 2009, he also joined the board of directors of the Web site Hunch.com. Hunch is a consumer Web application that uses information about people to suggest others things that they might like based on their known interests. Wales was also a former cochair of the World Economic Forum on the Middle East in 2008. His involvement in this forum might not immediately seem to fit his credentials quite as well as the others. However, the theme of this particular World Economic Forum was "Learning from the Future." Wales was able to offer insight on how the world may evolve in the next fifteen or twenty years based on his knowledge of how the world is changing the way information is spread today.

In his personal life, there have been changes, too. Wales and his wife, Christine, separated, although during their marriage they had one daughter, Kira. In 2011, the *Guardian* announced that Wales was engaged to Tony Blair's former secretary, Kate Garvey, whom he met while in Switzerland. While considering moving to England to be with Garvey, he also plans to regularly return to his current home in St. Petersburg, Florida, to visit his daughter.

In addition to his other work on various boards and committees, Wales is a public speaker who can be hired for

Wales is involved in organizations outside of Wikipedia. He was a cochair at the World Economic Forum in Egypt in 2008. The theme of the summit was "Learning from the Future."

speaking engagements on a variety of topics. He also participated in an ad campaign for Maurice Lacroix, a Swiss company that makes watches.

HARVESTING PROFITS ON THE WIKI FARM

One of Wales's biggest post-Wikipedia projects is very much connected to Wiki. It is a private company called Wikia that he founded with Angela Beesely, a former member of the Communications Committee for the Wikimedia Foundation. The company, which Wales helped found in 2004, is, unlike what Wikipedia has become, a for-profit company. The company was originally called Wikicities, but Wales decided that it was too confusing because people thought it was a city guide, so the name was changed to the simpler Wikia. So what does Wikia actually do? Wikia is a free Web hosting service for different wikis, or collections of information on a specific topic. Wikia and other free hosting services are sometimes referred to as wiki farms. In essence, it is a place where people with similar interests can compile information on a topic. If you like knitting, there is a wiki where a group of knitters creates a community with patterns and advice on knitting and crocheting. If you like food trucks, there is a wiki of people who review and discuss different food trucks and where they can be found. Basically, if there is an interest you have, there is likely a wiki for it. And if there isn't, you can start one on Wikia.

Wikia makes money in much the same way Bomis did in the beginning. In exchange for hosting these pages, which are normally free of charge for readers and editors, Wikia posts ads and makes most of its profit from advertising. Wikia hosts several hundred thousand wikis using open-source software similar to that of Wikipedia. Wales stepped down as the head of Wikia in 2009 but maintains the honorary title chairman emeritus, much as he does for the board of directors for the Wikimedia Foundation.

AWARDS AND HONORS

Wales has received a great deal of praise and many honors for his contributions to technology, the Internet, and the world at large. In 2006, Wales was listed in the "Scientists & Thinkers" section of *TIME* magazine's list of top one hundred people who are transforming the world. In 2007, he was twelve on *Forbes* magazine's list of Internet celebrities known as the "the Web Celebs 25." In 2010, Wales was again honored when he was chosen to give a lecture as part of the Stuart Regen Visionary series at the New Museum. The series of lectures is intended to honor "special individuals who have made major contributions to art and culture, and are actively imagining a better future." Although not strictly related to his work with Wikipedia, in April 2011, Wales was given the chance to serve on the jury of the world renowned Tribeca Film Festival.

Wales has received an Electronic Frontier Foundation Pioneer Award. This award is given out annually to people who have made significant contributions to the way people use computers and digital information. He also received the Gottlieb Duttweiler Prize from the institute of the same name. The award was given to him for making access to information more democratic and free for everyone. He also won the Monaco Media Prize and traveled to Monaco to accept it. Before founding Wikipedia, Wales had never been out of North America, and now he travels internationally at a nearly constant rate in order to keep up with the international community surrounding Wikipedia. In 2009, he received the Nokia Foundation annual award, again for his contributions to the evolution of the World Wide Web and making access to information freer and more available to all. Wales also won the Business Process Award at the 7th Annual Innovation Awards and Summit by the *Economist* for his business model allowing public collaboration and volunteers to complete a large-scale undertaking. Wales also won the Global Brand Icon of the Year Award in the award's second year of being bestowed. The only person to previously receive this distinguished award was Al Gore, who went on to win the Nobel Peace Prize in 2007. On behalf of the Wikimedia Foundation, Wales won the Quadriga Award, which is an annual German award sponsored by a nonprofit organization based in Berlin, Germany. This particular award recognizes four people each year for their commitment to innovation in political, economic, and cultural activities.

Wales has also received honorary degrees from colleges and universities all over the world, including Knox College, Amherst College, and Stevenson University in the United States, the Universidad Empresarial Siglo in Argentina, and MIREA University in Russia. Not a bad collection to add to the long list of schools he attended in his early life. His honorary degrees more than make up for the business Ph.D.s he chose not to complete in his twenties.

Wales has a number of published works, starting with the options pricing paper he wrote in grad school, which was published in a scholarly journal in 1999. More recently, he wrote the forward to several best-selling books dealing with the Internet or social networking. He has also published a number of articles in such places as the *Wall Street Journal* and *Advertising Age*. He also keeps a Web blog, which he occasionally updates with information on what

Wales has received a number of honors and awards for his work on Wikipedia and the Wikimedia Foundation. In 2008, he won the Quadriga Award, seen here, in the "Mission of Enlightenment" category.

he's up to, as well as his thoughts on the Internet, media, politics, and the spread of information. The tagline for this blog is fittingly "free knowledge for free minds." For more frequent updates on his thoughts, Wales keeps a Twitter account, which he updates many times daily.

But for all his awards and honors, it is hard to think that Jimmy Wales could have any more lasting legacy than the site for which he is best known. Wikipedia has truly revolutionized the world. It has made the sum of the world's knowledge free to anyone and proven that a volunteer-run collaboration is possible and can create something truly amazing. From a young boy thumbing through the *World Book Encyclopedia* in Huntsville, Alabama, to the dynamic individual who gave the world Wikipedia, Jimmy Wales has truly realized his vision. With no signs of slowing down, it is exciting to think what new visions Wales may have yet to realize and what world-changing projects he might come up with.

Fact Sheet on
Jimmy Wales

Full name: Jimmy Donnal Wales

Nickname: Jimbo

Date of birth: August 7, 1966

Birthplace: Huntsville, Alabama

Current residence: St. Petersburg, Florida

Marital status: Divorced (twice)

Children: One daughter, Kira, from marriage to wife Christine Rohan

Colleges attended: Auburn University (undergrad)

University of Alabama (master's in finance)

Indiana University at Bloomington (master's in finance)

First job: Chicago Options Associates

Titles held: President of Wikia, Inc. (2004–present)

Chairman of the Wikimedia Foundation (2003–2006)

Chairman Emeritus of the Wikimedia Foundation (2006–present)

WIKIPEDIA

Date launched: January 15, 2001

Slogan: The Free Encyclopedia

Founded by: Jimmy Wales and Larry Sanger

Operated under: Bomis, Inc. (2001–2003)

Wikimedia Foundation (2003–present)

Annual revenue: Nonprofit

Headquarters: San Francisco, California (Wikimedia Foundation)

Number of volunteers: 350,000

Number of employees: 75 (Wikimedia Foundation)

Number of articles: 19.7 million

Number of language editions: 282

Alexa rank: 6 (as of October 2011)

Timeline

August 7, 1966 Jimmy Wales is born in Huntsville, Alabama.

1979 Wales's parents enroll him in the prestigious Randolph School.

1982 Graduates high school and enrolls in Auburn University at the age of sixteen.

1986 Graduates from Auburn with a degree in finance. Marries first wife, Pam.

1988 Completes master's degree in finance at the University of Alabama.

1992 Wales leaves Indiana University without completing a doctorate. Moves to Chicago, Illinois, and gets a job at Chicago Options Associates as a trader.

1993 Wales and first wife, Pam, divorce.

1996 With partner Tim Shell, Wales founds Bomis, Inc.

1997 Marries second wife, Christine Rohan.

1998 Wales and his wife move to San Diego, California. Wales quits Chicago Options Associates to run Bomis full-time.

March 2000 With partner Larry Sanger, Wales launches Internet encyclopedia Nupedia.

January 15, 2001 The launch of Wikipedia.

2002 Wales and his family (wife and daughter Kira) move from San Diego to St. Petersburg, Florida.

June 20, 2003 Wales founds a nonprofit called the Wikimedia Foundation and becomes chairman of its board of directors.

2004 With partner Angela Beesley, Wales founds wiki hosting Web site for profit: Wikia, Inc.

2006 Wales steps down as CEO of Wikia and continues to hold an honorary position on its board as well as the board of the Wikimedia Foundation.

2008 Wales speaks at the World Economic Forum, recognized as one of the Young Global Leaders of 2007.

2009 Wales wins the annual award from the Nokia Foundation.

2011 Wales receives the Gottlieb Duttweiler Prize for his commitment to free information.

Glossary

computer programming Creating a sequence of instructions that tells a computer how to do something.

cyberspace The Internet; where electronic communication happens.

database A comprehensive collection of related data.

dissertation A long paper that is written in order to earn certain graduate degrees.

dot-com A company that does business mostly on the Internet.

emeritus Referring to a person who has retired from a position but still holds an honorary title.

host In relation to the Internet, to host means to run a site on the Internet.

institution An established foundation, often of an educational nature.

license Official permission to do or not do something.

message board A place on the Internet where people can communicate with others by posting messages.

Montessori school A school that follows an approach to education with emphasis on building children's independence.

nonprofit An organization that does a job without intending to make money.

NPOV Neutral point of view; a tenet of Wikipedia that it should be free from bias.

objectivism A philosophy created by writer Ayn Rand that states that there is an objective reality.

open source Practice of leaving the original source freely available to be redistributed with or without changes.

options pricing theory A theory of finance dealing with the trading of options.

piranha effect The idea that people in the Wikipedia community will gather in a feeding frenzy around incomplete articles.

public domain A term applied to things that can be used freely by anyone, which belong to the world.

software The programs used by a computer.

stub An incomplete article on Wikipedia.

trader A person whose job is to trade stocks, bonds, options, or futures.

troll In Internet-speak, a person who says things intentionally to upset people.

vandal Someone who causes intentional damage.

wiki An editable Web page, from a Hawaiian word for "quick."

wiki farm A site where a number of wikis are hosted.

wikitorial An editorial that can be edited by anyone.

Y2K The belief that computers would stop working at the beginning of the year 2000.

For More Information

Auburn University

Quad Center

Auburn, AL 36849-5111

(334) 844-4000

Web site: http://www.auburn.edu

Auburn University is a four-year public university in Alabama and is the school where Wales spent the years 1982–1986. He graduated from the university with an undergraduate degree in finance. The school is proud to claim Wales as an alumnus, and Wales has been written about in its school paper, the *Auburn Plainsmen.*

Berkman Center for Internet & Society

23 Everett Street, 2nd Floor

Cambridge, MA 02138

(617) 495-7547

Web site: http://cyber.law.harvard.edu

The Berkman Center is part of Harvard University, and its mission is to explore and understand the Internet. It is primarily a research center, of which Jimmy Wales is a member. Its Web site maintains a catalog of articles about Wales and his work on the Internet.

Creative Commons
444 Castro Street, Suite 900
Mountain View, CA 94041
Web site: http://www.creativecommons.org
Creative Commons is a nonprofit devoted to cataloging and distributing work that is made free to use by its creators. Jimmy Wales has served on the board of directors of Creative Commons since 2006, and its Web site maintains a short biography of him.

Gottlieb Duttweiler Institute
Langhaldenstrasse 21
P.O. Box 531
CH-8803 Rüschlikon/Zurich
Switzerland
Web site: http://www.gdi.ch/en
The Gottlieb Duttweiler Institute is a nonprofit foundation set up for the purpose of conducting scientific research in social and economic fields. The institute gives out a prize called the Gottlieb Duttweiler Prize to people who have made outstanding contributions to the global community. Jimmy Wales won this prize in 2011.

Indiana University at Bloomington
107 South Indiana Avenue
Bloomington, IN 47405
(812) 855-4848

Web site: http://www.iub.edu

Indiana University at Bloomington is a public research university in Bloomington, Indiana. It is here that Jimmy Wales studied for (but did not complete) a Ph.D. in finance. He also published a paper called "The Pricing of Index Options When the Underlying Assets All Follow a Lognormal Diffusion."

TED Conferences
250 Hudson Street, Suite 1002
New York, NY 10013
(212) 346-9333
Web site: http://www.ted.com

TED is a nonprofit organization that began in 1984 devoted to "ideas worth spreading" in technology, entertainment, and design. The organization has a twenty-minute video of Jimmy Wales speaking about the founding of Wikipedia on its site.

University of Alabama
Box 870100
Tuscaloosa, AL
(205) 348-6010
Web site: http://www.ua.edu

The University of Alabama is where Jimmy Wales earned his first master's degree in finance. It is also where he honed his philosophical and political interests.

Wikia, Inc.

500 3rd Street, Suite 405

San Francisco, CA 94107

Web site: http://www.wikia.com

Wikia is a collaborative publishing platform that enables people from all over the world to create and share content on almost any subject. It was founded by Jimmy Wales and Angela Beesley in 2004. Wales continues to serve with the honorary title of chairman emeritus on the board of directors.

Wikimedia Foundation

149 New Montgomery Street, 3rd Floor

San Francisco, CA 94105

(415) 839-6885

Web site: http://wikimediafoundation.org

The Wikimedia Foundation is a nonprofit organization dedicated to the distribution of multilingual text and visual content free of charge to people all over the world. The organization began in 2003 and is best known for its operating of the Web site Wikipedia.

World Economic Forum

United States Headquarters

3 East 54th Street, 18th Floor

New York, NY 10022

(212) 703-2300

Web site: http://www.weforum.org

The World Economic Forum is an independent organization that is committed to improving business, politics, and economics on a global scale. It honored Jimmy Wales as one of its "Young Global Leaders" in 2007, and he spoke at a conference in 2008. It maintains a short biography of Wales on its Web site.

WEB SITES

Due to the changing nature of Internet links, Rosen Publishing has developed an online list of Web sites related to the subject of this book. This site is updated regularly. Please use this link to access the list:

http://www.rosenlinks.com/ibio/wales

For Further Reading

Andersen, George. *Wikipedia: A Wikifocus Book.* San Francisco, CA: Wikifocus Books, 2011.

Ayers, Phoebe, Charles Matthews, and Ben Yates. *How Wikipedia Works: And How You Can Be a Part of It.* San Francisco, CA: No Starch Press Inc., 2008.

Barrett, Daniel J. *MediaWiki.* Sebastopol, CA: O'Reilly Media, 2009.

Berry, David. *Copy, Rip, Burn: The Politics of Copyleft and Open Source.* London, England: Pluto Books, 2008.

Borgman, Christine L. *Scholarship in the Digital Age: Information, Infrastructure, and the Internet.* Boston, MA: The MIT Press, 2010.

Broughton, John. *Wikipedia: The Missing Manual.* Sebastopol, CA: O'Reilly Media, 2008.

Dalby, Andrew. *The World and Wikipedia: How We Are Editing Reality.* London, England: Siduri Books, 2009.

Dibona, Chris, Mark Stone, and Danese Cooper. *Open Sources 2.0: The Continuing Evolution.* Sebastopol, CA: O'Reilly Media, 2005.

Hasan, Heather. *Wikipedia, 3.5 Million Articles & Counting: Using and Assessing the People's Encyclopedia.* New York, NY: Rosen Publishing, 2012.

Lessig, Lawrence. *Code and Other Laws of Cyberspace.* New York, NY: Basic Books, 2006.

Lessig, Lawrence. *Free Culture: The Nature and Future of Creativity.* New York, NY: Penguin, 2005.

Lih, Andrew. *The Wikipedia Revolution: How a Bunch of Nobodies Created the World's Greatest Encyclopedia.* New York, NY: Hyperion, 2009.

Mangu-Ward, Katherine. "Wikipedia and Beyond: Jimmy Wales' Sprawling Vision." *Reason*, June 1, 2007.

O'Sullivan, Dan. *Wikipedia.* Surrey, England: Ashgate Publishing Ltd., 2009.

Reagle, Joseph Michael. *Good Faith Collaboration: The Culture of Wikipedia.* Boston, MA: The MIT Press, 2010.

Wales, Jimmy. "Wikipedia Founder Jimmy Wales on Making the Most of Company Wikis." *Harvard Business Review*, March 3, 2009.

Weber, Steven. *The Success of Open Source.* Cambridge, MA: Harvard University Press, 2005.

Wu, Tim. *The Master Switch: The Rise and Fall of Information Empires.* Toronto, ON, Canada: Alfred A. Knopf, 2010.

Bibliography

Bergstein, Brian. "Sanger Says He Co-started Wikipedia." MSNBC, March 25, 2007. Retrieved September 9, 2011 (http://www.msnbc.msn.com/id/17798723).

Harry Walker Agency. "Jimmy Wales Complete Bio" Retrieved August 7, 2011 (http://www.harrywalker. com/bios/Wales_Jimmy.pdf).

Kansas City infoZine News. "EFF Honors Craigslist, Gigi Sohn, and Jimmy Wales with Pioneer Awards." April 28, 2006. Retrieved August 7, 2011 (http://www. infozine.com/news/stories/op/storiesView/sid/14632).

Kazek, Kelly. "Wikipedia Founder, Huntsville Native, Jimmy Wales, Finds Fame 'Really Cool.'" *News Courier* (Athens, Alabama), August 12, 2006. Retrieved August 9, 2011 (http://enewscourier.com/x1037404066/ Wikipedia-founder-Huntsville-native-Jimmy-Wales-finds-fame-really-cool?keyword=leadpicturestory).

Lamb, Brian. Chat transcript with Jimmy Wales. Q & A, September 25, 2005. Retrieved August 20, 2011 (http:// www.q-and-a.org/Transcript/?ProgramID=1042).

Lih, Andrew. *The Wikipedia Revolution: How a Bunch of Nobodies Created the World's Greatest Encyclopedia.* New York, NY: Hyperion, 2009.

Olson, Parmy. "A New Kid on the Wiki Block." Forbes.com, October 18, 2006 (http://www.forbes.com/2006/10/18/sanger-wikipedia-citizendium-face-cx_po_1018autofacescan02.html).

Pink, Daniel H. "The Book Stops Here." *Wired*, Issue 13:03, March 2005. Retrieved August 7, 2011 (http://www.wired.com/wired/archive/13.03/wiki.html?pg=3&topic=wiki&topic_set=).

Sanger, Larry. "The Early History of Nupedia and Wikipedia: A Memoir." Slashdot.com. Retrieved September 12, 2011 (http://features.slashdot.org/story/05/04/18/164213/the-early-history-of-nupedia-and-wikipedia-a-memoir).

Smith, Wes. "He's the 'God-King,' But You Can Call Him Jimbo." *Seattle Times*, January 15, 2007. Retrieved August 9, 2011 (http://seattletimes.nwsource.com/html/businesstechnology/2003525473_btwikipedia15.html).

Wales, Jimmy. "Foreword," in Andrew Lih, *The Wikipedia Revolution: How a Bunch of Nobodies Created the World's Greatest Encyclopedia*. First ed. New York, NY: Hyperion, 2009.

Wales, Jimmy, and Andrea Weckerle. "Foreword," in Matthew Fraser and Soumitra Dutta, *Throwing Sheep in the Boardroom: How Online Social Networking Will Transform Your Life, Work and World*. First ed. New York, NY: Wiley, 2008

Index

ABOUT THE AUTHOR

Susan Meyer is a writer working in the children's educational publishing market. She has written several books for Rosen Publishing. Meyer lives in Queens, New York.

PHOTO CREDITS